WHY DO BULLIES BULLY?

AND WHAT WE CAN DO ABOUT IT!

by Sherry Skramstad

River Boat Books

This edition is published by River Boat Books, St. Paul, MN; and it is printed in the United States of America.

First printing August 12, 2023.
ISBN: 978-1-955823-14-2

Information related to Pennsylvania statutes regarding bullying was forward to the author from the Office of Pennsylvania State Representative Thom Welby, and from Drew Popish, the Chief of Staff for State Representative Bridget Kozierowski.

Cover artwork was adapted from a street painting created by Kid Habibi, Grafitti and Street Artist, New York, New York.

Praise for Sherry Skramstad and her book *Wendy's Wisdom*, which has now been reissued as *The Lucky Few*

"The engaging, emotionally vibrant and uncompromisingly honest story of two sisters who shared a fundamental belief in human values. That one of them had Down Syndrome seems almost beside the point. In Sherry Skramstad's deeply felt and sharply-etched memoir, the sisters reveal themselves as supplemental to each other, celebrating their differences rather than merely accepting them or pretending they do not exist. To read this book is to feel a lot better about the human race. A wonderful story, full of surprises, that is a pleasure to read." – Hesh Kestin, author of *Based on a True Story* and *The Iron Will of Shoeshine Cats*.

"Sherry Skramstad's *Wendy's Wisdom* is masterful; taking readers on a voyage of discovery they'll remember their entire lives. For not only do we learn of her incredible sister, who never let Down Syndrome prevent her from enjoying life every day, but we also learn about ourselves. {Are we the ones who laugh cruelly at those who are different from us; do we ignore them, or do we treat them as human beings?} Too often, the greatest obstacle for a person who is handicapped is how other people perceive them. Reading *Wendy's Wisdom* may challenge your perceptions and your values. We can only thank Wendy for doing that. ... {Brilliant!}"

–Bill Heller, author of *After The Finish Line: The Race To End Horse Slaughter In America, Saratoga Tales, Playing Tall; The Ten Shortest Players In NBA History* and *Randy Romero's Remarkable Life.*

"A poignant story of devotion, sisterhood and life's unexpected 'victories.' And it's all true!"

–Len Berman, Sportscaster, *Spanning The World* WNBC TV Sports (retired); Creator, len@lenbermansports.com, and author of *The Greatest Moments In Sports.*

"Down syndrome is simply another barrier to success, and was nearly a death sentence as recently as fifty years ago. *Wendy's Wisdom: The Challenges and Accomplishments of a Woman with Down Syndrome* is written by special education teacher Sherry Skramstad as she remembers her sister, Wendy, who faced (being born with) Down syndrome in the 1940s. Telling the story of what those with Down syndrome go through and what they can accomplish, *Wendy's Wisdom* is a devoted study, highly recommended."

–Midwest Book Review, – May 7, 2011 (Oregon, WI USA)

"Sherry Skramstad's insightful book goes to the heart of the emotions and issues faced by siblings of people with developmental disabilities. Wendy and Sherry shared a warm, witty, wonderful journey through life, despite the obstacles that Down Syndrome erected along the way. {....A wonderful experience.....Very engaging.}"

–Renee Kaplan, former Events Desk Editor, Newsday

"Sherry Skramstad's wonderful new book, *Wendy's Wisdom*, is not only an inspiring tribute to her sister, a Down Syndrome survivor, but also a loving portrait of two sisters growing up in mid-century Brooklyn. You will learn more about horses, roulette, the Catskills and real family values from this impressive first work. Read it and feel good."

–David Hoffman, Chief Librarian, *Newsday*

"Sherry Skramstad tells a wonderful story of sisterhood in her book, *Wendy's Wisdom*. As a mom of a child with Down syndrome, Sherry opened a door for me; sharing insights on the sibling relationship. Sherry expected nothing short of the typical sibling bond and Wendy gave it right back. No preconceived ideas or limitations affected the relationship. It is a triumph of the human spirit."

–Gail Williamson, Executive Director, Down Syndrome Association of Los Angeles,

, Inc.;Creator of DSIAM, a one stop place for producers and directors seeking actors and actresses with Down syndrome

"I feel privileged to have known Wendy and to have been her friend. She had a unique way of expressing herself and never hesitated when she thought it was called for. I think we are all indebted to Sherry Skramstad for acquainting us with Wendy and I truly believe that this book should be required reading for all of us who think of ourselves as thoughtful human beings. There's a lot to learn here."

–David Bennett Cohen, member of the band *Country Joe and the Fish,* and also *The Blues Project*; also was the hed pianist for the Broadway musical *Rent*

Acknowledgements

I offer a hearty thank you to my good friends Maggie LoRusso, Ray Daniels, Agnes Golo and Terese Searfoss for their kind attention and valuable opinions on the first draft of this handbook. I also offer my deep gratitude to Professor Jeff Welsh and Principal Matt Montoro for their suggestions that vastly improved the information collected for this work.

Additionally, I am sincerely grateful to Congressman Matt Cartwright and his staff for providing me with the statistics on the rise of teenage suicide since the influence of the internet on our society within two days of my request. Similarly, I must thank state representatives Bridget Kozierowski and Thom Welby and their staffs for supplying me with the current laws that exist against bullying in Pennsylvania public schools as listed on the pages following this one.

State Representative Kyle Mullins met with me in his office to review what I had already written in this handbook. In that meeting, Representative Mullins seemed quite impressed with the fact that this handbook offered a six-step approach to address bullying. He had already introduced anti-bullying legislation in the Pennsylvania House of Representatives and is currently engaged with a woman who formed an anti-bullying organization. He was especially taken with the fact that in this handbook, student peers were the first to address alleged incidents of bullying. He said he had never heard of that before but thought it was an excellent suggestion. He told me that he intends to introduce this handbook to the Deputy of Education in the state of Pennsylvania.

And lastly, I must thank my Editor and Publisher, Peter Damian Bellis, for requiring more research and for making this handbook more cohesive and more easily readable.

To Wendy,
who taught me respect for values and differences

CONTENTS

WHY DO BULLIES BULLY?

AND WHAT WE CAN DO ABOUT IT!

What I Have Learned About Bullies

The truth about bullies is that they feel inferior. Every single one of them. They feel the need to pick on others because it makes them feel better about themselves. This comes about as they learn to compare themselves to others; be it siblings when they are younger or to classmates once they enter school. I believe the main goal of a bully is to impress their peers so that if others think of them as more powerful than they truly feel, their own analysis of themselves will improve. That's why I believe involving the peers of students who bully others is the crucial concept in teaching bullies not only to respect others, and to tolerate difference; but to address their own needs regarding themselves.

What Do Young People Need In Order To Feel Good About Who They Are?

For the most part I believe young people need to feel accepted by family and peers.

They need to feel appreciated for who they are, what they believe and the role they play in other's lives. I believe they need to feel important or significant to someone. And I believe they need to feel a sense of purpose in their lives.

Just how does a youngster develop these feelings in order to become a well adjusted, self confident person? Usually, they feel that they contribute to some group (family, class, etc.). Having responsibility and someone counting on them for their contribution (washing dishes, cleaning one's room, baby sitting, shopping) makes them feel important and a part of something. Adopting goals gives them a sense of purpose and can earn them respect.

My Early Experiences with a Bully

I learned about bullying behavior early in my life. My mother divorced my father after his return from WWII and married a man whose first child was born with Down Syndrome in 1948 when I was just six years old. Perhaps because of the difference between my sister and myself or perhaps because my stepfather's family disowned him for marrying a woman who already had a child, my stepfather threatened me with physical harm, embarrassed me in front of others, insulted my looks and my intelligence and at times, beat me. He basically made my early life a living hell. If he called my name or tapped me on the shoulder (hard), I literally trembled in fear. After my sister was born, other children from our apartment building, whom I considered friends at the time, made fun of her looks. That led me to my very first lesson in choosing friends. After expressing my concerns to another, older girl from our apartment building, Miriam told me that if the girls I knew were that mean to a new born baby then they weren't worthy of being considered my fiends. What a valuable lesson to learn at the age of six.

One thought I'd like to add about my early relationship with my stepfather regards a movie I saw on television when I was about eleven years old. I learned many morals from movies, as neither my mother nor my stepfather ever counseled me on moral behavior.

In the movie, a teenage boy was bullied by a male adult. His response was not to show any emotion. Since the object of bullying appears to be gaining evidence that the bully has power over someone they deem less powerful, the refusal of the target to demonstrate any emotion robs the bully of the desired effect.

The boy in the movie wouldn't cry. He wouldn't talk back. He wouldn't defend himself. He just wouldn't respond! When his friend in the movie asked him why he wouldn't respond to being bullied, the boy said, "I will never show him that what he says bothers me! I will never let him think that he has any power over me!"

What an epiphany that was for me! How simple and how intelligent! That very moment I decided that I would adopt that non response the very next time my stepfather bullied or insulted or even hit me.

The next time he shouted at me, I stared straight up into his face.

At first that shocked and then *infuriated* him. He was losing his power over me!

He slapped my face.

I stared back! I refused to cry as I had in the past.

He didn't know what to do! I had stolen his power over me!

Then he walked away from me, shaking his head.

I had just learned a valuable lesson, though at the time I was still too timid to talk back to him for fear of getting a real beating.

I used this lesson at various times throughout my life; when I tried not to allow anyone to assume they held any power over me.

Several times in my life I have been threatened by others who sought to bully me and each instance produced a revelation that I used in later life, especially during the thirty three years I spent as a teacher of students with special needs, both in public schools and in two New York State prisons.

How Should We Respond To A Bully?

When I was a fifth-grader, I often played with a Spalding ball in the school yard during recess. I wasn't paying attention to anything but the ball. But one day, my ball rolled into the path of a sixth-grade girl named Leslie and interrupted what she was doing, she approached me and asked me why I bothered her.

At a time when most girls wore skirts to school, Leslie had a reputation of being a "tomboy" who wore jeans and sweat shirts and generally tried to threaten other children; girls or boys. I protested my innocence to her; saying my disturbance of her school yard activity had not been intentional. This did not seem to satisfy what she considered an interference with her activity and she told me to meet her the next morning at the entrance to the corner store on the street where the school was located and she told me to be there half an hour before school started.

I was afraid of her. I was afraid she might "beat me up", as she had had several fights in school before this episode. Still, I went to meet her. I don't know. Perhaps it was because I was already so afraid of disobeying my stepfather that it was ingrained in me to not dispute directions from those in what seemed to be a superior position of power. Perhaps I was just curious to see what would transpire. Or maybe, she just didn't scare me as much as my stepfather did; so no matter what she'd say or do, it couldn't compare to what he did to me. I believe that was a recurring theme throughout my life. Or possibly, it was because I inherently knew that to grant power to others over your own life, was wrong.

On the day I met Leslie at the store before school started, she asked me why I hadn't been afraid to meet her. I shrugged and said that I agreed to meet her the day before and that I didn't go against what I had already agreed to do. Leslie looked stunned. Evidently, this meant something significant to her as she put her arm around my shoulder and said that if anyone in school ever bothered me I should tell her and she'd take care of it.

That was my "Leslie" lesson. The outcome encouraged me to face what might be frightening but could lead to an unlikely surprise.

Like my "Miriam" lesson, it got included in
what I later used to guide my adult behavior.

Applying What I Learned In My Own Classes

During my first year as a special educator,
I taught middle school kids. One of my duties
was to visit with the parents of each student,
along with the student, to create an individual
education plan.

One of my students lived in a low-income
apartment complex in an area that had a
rough reputation. There was no father in
his home, and his mother never left her
apartment. She was so heavy that she couldn't
climb or descend stairs or walk unassisted.
When I arrived at the complex, a tall teenager
accosted me and asked me what I was doing
there. I realized immediately that he was
attempting to challenge and probably frighten
me. But I was not phased. I just took the time
to look around the complex, from building to
buidling to the grassy area in the mdidle with
some old playground equipment, and then I
simply said, "This looks nice. Maybe I'll move
in here."

The young man looked surprised at first
and then he smiled and said, "Oh, you're
probably somebody's teacher!"

I smiled and said, "Yep!"

For some reason, his challenge didn't scare me. I felt perfectly comfortable in that space. Evidently, Not appearing intimidated by him earned respect from him for me.

I got to love those twelve- to fourteen-year old-students in my first year of teaching middle school and I've kept in touch with some of them for many years. Among them was a thin, scrawny, fourteen-year-old boy named Joe, with pimples on his face and seemingly infected blackheads in his ears.

I looked forward to meeting his family when we had our first quarterly individual education plan meeting. I thought I'd bring up the subject of working on personal hygiene. This young man was less outgoing than most of the other students in the class; and not as quick to learn as most of them, but I never heard any of the others taunt him in any way.

About a month into the school year, a recent Hispanic refugee girl named Maria, was placed in our class. She didn't speak English, and perhaps because of it, she was very shy. At the first sight of this girl, who may have appeared to have more problems than Joe, he began to pick on her. He made fun of the fact that she couldn't make herself understood. He'd point at her and make fun of the clothes she was wearing. Joe had finally found someone he thought had less status in the class than himself.

I told Joe his shaming of the new girl wasn't acceptable and I couldn't wait for the individual education plan meeting with Joe's parent.

Was I in for a surprise!

Joe's father showed up in dirty work clothes at the time for the planned meeting but when we began to fill out the paperwork necessary for what Joe would work on for the next three months, I realized Joe's father was illiterate. He couldn't read; not even as well as Joe.

Joe's mother had died when he was quite young, his father told me; so Joe was left with no one at home to help him with hygiene or academics or acceptable social behavior. I decided that Joe's progress in all realms of life (except financial support) was up to me.

Despite my admonishments, Joe continued to make fun of Maria in class. She looked confused because she couldn't understand exactly what he said but from the frowns of the others in the class, I think she realized that he was making fun of her. He certainly didn't demonstrate any signs of welcoming her.

I told Joe it wasn't right: that his bullying wasn't acceptable. I asked him how he would feel if others in the class made fun of him. I even asked him if he ever washed inside his ears.

I used sympathy. I told Joe I could imagine how hard it could be to grow up without a mother.

I used logic; telling him that others wouldn't like him if he continued to behave this way.

I did everything I could think of, short of punishing him, to get him to stop making fun of Maria. Nothing worked. So I decided punishment might be the only solution. Every day that Joe said something derogatory to or about Maria, I kept him after school.

Joe's After-School Punishment

I always wrote my lesson plans after school. You would see me in my classroom, gathering whatever materials I thought I would need for the next day's lessons. I might be there till five o'clock. But now Joe was right there with me. So I gave him some extra tutoring in the reading workbook we used in class. I asked him to write what he had done wrong that day. I asked him to write down what he could have done instead and I checked his work before I left for home. I couldn't tell if Joe liked the extra attention or the opportunity to learn more or if he was ashamed to be kept after school or if he minded my interference with his plans for the rest of the day.

I thought Joe's punishment might last two weeks. I was sure Joe would get tired of staying late every day after school. But his bullying behavior lasted for months! Just before Christmas, when I was about to give up and tell him the punishment wasn't working, Joe stopped insulting Maria and making fun of her. When I asked him why he had stopped bothering Maria, his response was simple.

"I got tired of staying late after school," he told me.

And I was just about to stop using that tactic!

Teaching In Prison

Later on in my life, when I was teaching Class A felony offenders (rapists, murderers and armed robbers) in a Division for Youth facility (for juveniles aged 14 to 21) in Goshen, NY, I explained to my pre-algebra class that math had never been my strong suite and that I was giving them homework to test whether or not my presentation of the material was sufficient for them to understand and master it correctly. If I learned from that that the correct solutions were too hard to produce, I would need to find another way to present the material. Most of the students didn't believe I was trying to help them. I think they always felt that it was them who were being judged.

The next morning I asked one of the students in the back row where his homework was. He said, "I never did homework out in

the world. You think I'm going to do it in
here, for you?"

I shrugged and said, "No matter to me. I'll
see you next semester for the same course; in
the same place."

He seemed infuriated by that; perhaps
because he'd have to repeat the course;
perhaps because I wasn't frightened by his
challenge.

"You know that woman in Connecticut,"
he said, "who had her throat slit from ear to
ear?" And then he moved his forefinger under
his chin from ear to ear.

I didn't know that woman but because I
wanted him to get to his point, I said,"Yeah,".

"I did that!"

So I responded in kind.

"So what is that supposed to make me do?
Quake in my boots?"

Immediately a huge grin broke out on his
face and he said, "That's what I love about
you 'Skrammie'! You have heart!"

I never meant my response to prove my
"heart". I worked in a place with a lot of
security, so it never dawned on me to be
afraid of an implied verbal threat in my class.
This young man went on to what the students
called, "The Big House" (a regular New
York State prison) when he was 21; which,
at that time, was only several months away

for him. From "The Big House" this former student wrote to me that I had changed his life. (Which I took to mean that I reformed his view of White women not being scared by Black men.)

After that confrontation in class, the other students asked me, "Where you from, teach?" Although I was living in upstate New York at the time, I was born in Brooklyn and had lived there for thirty-six years. When I told the students I had grown up in Brooklyn, there was an audible, "Ahhhhh! Brooklyn!"

At the time I thought their reaction strange; as though having lived in Brooklyn explained my not appearing to be frightened by implied threats. Upon further reflection, perhaps my having been born and growing up in Brooklyn, and having been exposed to all its diversity, did make me unafraid of what others may have feared. I know it definitely separated me from the other White female teachers who also taught there and had grown up in upstate New York that did not have much of that same diversity.

Another incident at that facility is worth mentioning. This time, over a physical threat. On a day when one of the more troublesome students at the prison was told he couldn't go to shop because the shop teacher was absent, he was assigned to my class for the period.

He was upset by that and went down the school corridor slamming the see through plastic window of every classroom he passed. I was standing at the front of my room, when he entered with a raised fist and came directly at me.

The noise he created in the corridor had alerted the Educational Supervisor (the equivalent of a Principal in a public school) and he was hiding out in the hall; crooking his finger at me as though telling me to run out of the classroom. Every student's eye was on me at the front of the room as this troubled young man kept approaching me with his fist raised. I knew that if I ran, I would never have the respect of any student in that classroom again. I could not risk my career by running, so I backed up against the desk believing it would brace me for whatever blow might be struck.

Just at the moment the student reached me, a security guard reached him and caught his arm and put it behind his back. I must say though, that this guard slowly and deliberately put his bagged lunch on top of the metal cabinet in the classroom and advanced on the student as he approached me, ever so slowly. The look of admiration on the faces of the other students in the class let me know that I had made the correct decision not to run.

Discovering My Power

Another "bullying" incident that impacted my life happened at Monticello Raceway when I was the Assistant Director of Publicity there at the age of forty two. My mother and stepfather owned several harness horses that they raced at the track. One Sunday afternoon, the two of them, my sisters Wendy and Valarie and I were having lunch in the dining room. At that time Wendy worked in a sheltered workshop and like my mother, she enjoyed gambling. She bet her own money and made her own selections. She was 36 at the time. Because her salary was not great from the sheltered workshop, Wendy *allowed* other people to bet with her on a ticket. Many people fought for that privilege as Wendy tended to be very lucky; at the track, at bingo, etc. (I often thought God was making up to her for the burden with which she was born.)

Wendy told me her pick for the next race (which was a long shot, as her picks often were. That's why it was so valuable to be her "partner".) and asked if I'd like to share the bet with her.

"Of course," I said. (Though it was not a choice I'd have made on my own).

As Wendy left to go to the window to place our bet, my stepfather said to her, "Bet it for show!"

Wendy resisted.

"I want to bet it to win." she said.

"I said, bet it for show!" my stepfather insisted.

Wendy went to the window grumbling all the way. Later, her pick came in to win at 44 to one; meaning that had she bet it to win, she and I would be splitting $90 for a $1 investment! But she had yielded to my stepfather's wishes though the only money that went through that teller's window was *her* dollar and *mine*! I still didn't know what bet Wendy had made but the show ticket she bought had us splitting only $14! Wendy was upset (as was I) and she kept mumbling under her breath, "Play it for shoooow. Play it for shoooow!"

My stepfather (probably because he felt guilty and was embarrassed by being one-upped by Wendy) started poking Wendy on the shoulder, as he had so often done to me. "What's the matter, Wendy?" he said. "You have a problem, Wendy?"

A lot of eyes in the dining room were now on our table. Wendy was blushing and obviously embarrassed. But he didn't stop poking and asking her the same questions over and over.

Though he had done that very same thing so often in the past to me, and I had responded exactly how Wendy was doing then, seeing it done to someone else, someone who had difficulties enough, I snapped!

"YES, she has a problem and *so do I*! That was *our* money we bet; not yours! How *dare* you tell her how to bet it? Are you going to make up the difference in what we lost?"

At this point my mother chimed in.

"Sherry, you're raising your voice. Other people are staring at us!", she said.

Then, my stepfather got up from the table and went to his box, reserved for horse owners. *He was now the one* who couldn't stand being embarrassed in public!

But I was incensed. I kept it up.

"How can he tell two grown women how to bet their own money? Who does he think he is?"

I knew I was upsetting my mother, so I got up from the table and started down the stairs to the parking lot; planning to leave the racetrack. But halfway down the steps, I asked myself what I was doing. My stepfather had humiliated both Wendy and me in public and I was allowing him to get away with it, *again*? This was *my* track! *I* worked here! *I* had friends here. So I marched back up the stairs and accosted my stepfather in the clubhouse; at his box seat.

"What's the matter, Sol? Can't take the heat? Why don't you come out here and solve things the way you always do? Why don't you come out here and hit me? C'mon Sol! Come out and hit me! Do in public what you always do in private. C'mon Sol!"

And I raised my fists in a boxing stance as though I was going to fight with him in the aisle.

A friend of my stepfather's and a trainer I knew from the racetrack put his arm around me. He whispered to me, "Class, Sherry. Have some class."

I looked him straight in the eye and said, "I think I've started to show some 'class' for the first time in my life!"

My stepfather slunk down in his seat. He looked as if he wanted to disappear.

I had done that! I had!

I had never realized that I had that kind of power! Then I hopped down the steps to the parking lot and got in my car. On the ramp to the highway on my way home I caught myself *singing at the top of my lungs*! I had finally faced the bully and *he was mine*!

It had taken me thirty-eight years to gain the courage to stand up to that particular bully and I was *upset* with myself for having waited so long. But from that day on, my life changed. I bought a farm, horses of my own, wrote a book, got divorced, changed jobs, sold my old car, and became the Director of Publicity and Public Relations at a major racetrack in the northeast. What being bullied at a young age can make you fear to attempt!

How I Used What I'd Learned

When I was teaching in my classroom several years later, I took what I had learned and offered it to my public middle school students. I taught them about Freud and about Adler's theory of compensation. I told them that those who feel the need to bully do not feel good about themselves. When others in the building would make fun of them at recess or whatever joint activity they had together, I told my students to ask of their tormentors, "Who made you feel so bad about yourself that you need to put me down to feel better about yourself?" Most of the time, the bully, realizing that his "front" had been torn away, just walked away silently; knowing that his secret had been discovered.

Having attended the City College of New York during the time it became Huey Newton College for several days, and during the time of the rise of the (original) Black Panthers, I saw how afros and dashikis and corn row gave Blacks an identity of which they were proud.

The way the Black Panthers embraced their heritage taught me a *most valuable* lesson. Take what others see as your weakness or your difference and *make it your strength!* As my high school biology teacher informed the class (though I guess I knew it all along *but not the significance of it*), "It is only those who are different from the status quo that lead to evolution!"

And that evolution could be biological as well as cultural! For example, the law regarding special education in New York State limits class size and a divided classroom between two separate classes with only a divider between them leaves students who have difficulty concentrating in the first place, at an even greater disadvantage.

To address this issue, another special educator and I got permission from the Principal to group the fifth- and sixth-grade special needs classes together. With each of our two classroom aides, we could have four reading groups and four math groups, each led by an adult in the same classroom.

The students never knew or obsessed about which level group they were in and they could move up or down as their individual needs dictated. Each group had sufficiently interesting material that all were actively involved in their learning.

We used Fearon classics for reading that were high interest low reading level but related the actual stories of, *Twenty Thousand Leagues Under The Sea*, *A Tale Of Two Cities*, etc. Students loved carrying their books in their back pockets with the titles sticking out so other students in the building could see what they were reading. They felt included.

In this classroom I taught my students about the theories of the great psychologists and we put a yellow banner diagonally across our classroom door. Since we had two special educators and two classroom aides in that room, we wrote the first initial of each adult's last name on that banner so that everyone who passed our door would ask, "What's in there? The inevitable answer was, "Oh, that's the special class!"

On occasion, when someone from another class (usually not the best of students) would taunt anyone from our class, upon learning of the incident, I would invite them into my classroom (with their teacher's permission, of course) and I would stand them at the front of the room and ask them about *Adler's Theory of Compensation*. I knew they didn't know and hadn't been taught that as part of their curriculum so when they couldn't answer I'd call on one of my students to explain it. We did the same with some tidbit of information about Freud or Jung and they would go back to their classes and tell their fellow students, "Boy, what a special class that is!"

So what is it that I have learned from all of these encounters with *would-be* bullies? I have learned that those who have confidence in themselves are not usually the ones who bully others. More often then not, they are the ones who seek to help others. Bullies really *do not* want others to perceive them as bad. They are happy when someone they attempt to bully sees the threat for what it is but does not take the bait to challenge them.

Bullies only pick on others they perceive as weaker than themselves in order to appear stronger or more capable to their peers that they see as more powerful or capable than themselves. When the threats of bullies are dismissed or not taken seriously and the potential targets are not fearful, then the bullies are allowed to believe in their own goodness; which is really they way they want to believe about themselves.

Leslie didn't want to been seen as feared by me. The teenager at the projects liked that I wasn't intimidated by him. My student at the Division For Youth was happy that I wasn't frightened by his implied threat. But when I directly fought back against my stepfather's bullying tactics, he sold all his horses and never went back to that racetrack again. I had reinforced his feeling that he really was inferior.

The fact that a man that had bullied a four year old stepdaughter and a developmentally challenged woman was so weak that he could be trounced by a former subject of his bullying only enhanced my stepfather's feelings of inferiority. So what is the real truth about bullies? They *ALL* feel inferior to others!

A Bully Named
Donald Trump

When I first conceived of this book, it was well in advance of Donald Trump's entrance to the Oval Office. I offer this section not as a judgment of his character or behavior but as a way of understanding how his feelings of inferiority as a youngster guided his later personality and decision making. I believe he developed those feelings of inferiority in elementary school.

After years of observing his behavior in office and having been a special educator for over three decades, I believe I totally understand the personality he developed. I'm convinced (as is easy to observe when Trump reads off the teleprompter) that when Donald Trump first attended elementary school, his dyslexia (reading letters of the alphabet backwards) went undiagnosed and untreated. Trump and I are about the same age, and at the time we both attended elementary school. dyslexia was not recognized, and therefore it was not addressed.

Without being able to keep up with others in his class because of his difficulty in reading, I believe a young Donald Trump felt inferior to the others in his class. Many students who do not fare well in class take to acting out, as they then receive the attention they crave. Whether it is attention for good or for bad is unimportant. One is still the object of attention and therefore *not* unimportant.

This allows students who feel inferior to *feel* important even if they don't feel capable. But the feelings of inferiority to others do not go away just because one receives attention. So those who feel inferior must *constantly* prove to themselves that they *are* important; significant enough to be recognized.

It is important to note that although students with feelings of inferiority to others may get the attention they seek with negative behaviors, that does nothing to assuage their feelings that they are "less than" the others among whom they find themselves. Often, not being recognized as as one of the "good students" makes poorer students develop what educators call *oppositional disorder*.

I believe it is this disorder that was probably expressed at home, as well as at school, when Donald was young, that prompted Fred Trump to send this particular son away to military school, where he felt Donald might learn discipline. The elder Trump never sent any of Donald's other three siblings away from home for schooling.

At military school, Donald saw the absolute authority of being at the top of a military chain of command. He aspired to have that same sense of control over everything in his environment. Hence, his obsession with "being at the top" and having *no one* question his authority. Hence also, his obsession with *the generals*. Yet, it is significant to note that although Trump attended military school and envied the authority of the generals, he never sought to enter any military service (and indeed, may have sought to avoid it).

To this day, Trump's continued difficulty in reading has prevented him from having an informed and accurate view of history. Nor do I believe he was clearly aware of the divisions among the three branches of the American government and the "checks and balances" written into the Constitution of the United States.

This continuing difficulty reading caused Trump's daily briefings as President to be boiled down to one page and sometimes even to maps and drawings. This limitation causes his impromptu diversions from his prepared speeches or reading from a teleprompter. It makes delivering security briefs to him almost impossible and makes him the butt of many jokes. At present, it adds to the question of, "Why would he steal government documents he couldn't even read or understand?" while he was President.

I think it is significant to add the report that the only book his first wife Ivana ever saw him attempt to read was *Mein Kampf,* which he kept on the night stand near his bed. However, I believe that she also said she never saw him actually reading it.

As an experienced teacher of students with special needs, I have long been curious about Donald Trump's grades in high school and in college. I have been intrigued by the fact that a person with such a severe and unaddressed reading disability could be as successful as Mr. Trump claimed to be throughout his years of higher education. He says he knows *many great words*, though his vocabulary appears extremely limited and tends mostly towards superlatives and hyperbole and is rarely specific.

Until recently I had not known that Mr. Trump had instructed his personal attorney, Michael Cohen, to write threatening letters to to his high school and colleges, warning them that should they ever reveal Donald Trump's grades, or his SAT score, they would be sued in civil and criminal court and possibly be exposed to other unwelcome actions.

As this information has now been made public in an open hearing by the House Oversight Committee, it will be interesting to see if these grades will be sought by Congress through subpoenas. The grades, themselves, may be interesting as well, should they ever be released.

In so many ways, the oppositional disorder, developed when a young Donald couldn't keep up with his class in reading, describes most all of Donald Trump's behavior: his comfort in the midst of the chaos he is constantly creating, his need for constant attention; his comfort with being at odds with all those around him and his need to seek *negative* attention.

How does one explain Donald Trump's apparent negative views of people who are of a different race, ethnicity, religion, etc. and *why* is he so obsessed about the country from which an American citizen's family came? One must remember that Donald Trump's father, Fred, immigrated from Germany at a time between World Wars I and II. He was exposed to the hateful rhetoric of Adolph

Hitler. Fred Trump was arrested as a participant in a Ku Klux Rally in Poughkeepsie in the early 1940s.

Donald was not only raised by his father, he worked with him for years in the older Trump's real estate empire when both were charged with unfair housing practices for denying rental apartments to Black people. Evidently, Fred passed on his prejudices to his son who has never renounced them. Having been so influenced by his father, Donald can not imagine that any other person would not be so influenced.

With regard to those die-hard Trump supporters whose loyalty knows no bounds despite whatever outrageous things Donald Trump may say or do, could it be because they identify in feeling inferior to others, as does Mr. Trump? Can the fact that these people are generally lacking in higher education lead them to feel inferior to others with more advanced educations and higher incomes? Could their loyalty to Trump be the result of recognizing his intellectual difficulties and seeing themselves in him?

If so, their continued support of Donald Trump may have more to do with looking down on immigrants as *less than* themselves. That may allow them to feel superior to someone rather than harboring an actual

The face of a bully who needs to
denounce others to feel better about himself.
(Photo by River Boat Books staff.)

fear of immigrants; which may be why their loyalty never wavers, despite so many realistic facts constantly being revealed about their idol. This response is typical of bullying behavior. It is also very reminiscent of the behavior of my student with the dirty ears.

As I already explained, I added this section on Donald Trump *NOT* as a judgment of him or his character, but as a way to understand how a young person can develop the need to bully others, as they see it; and since, as a former President of the United States, Trump and his behaviors are universally known, so using him as an example can be understood by so many.

I present this theory about Trump's behavior because so many Americans are aware of how he behaves. One cannot watch him at a rally, whether in person or through the lens of a television news clip, and *NOT* witness him acting like a bully. So it makes intuitive sense to understand this behavior as an example of someone who feels the need to bully others in order to feel better about themselves.

Once Trump became President, like the generals at the military school he attended, he felt there was no one who could over rule whatever he chose to do. I believe it was so difficult for him to admit that he had lost his re-election because that meant that others saw his weaknesses and his entire life had been spent attempting to cover them up. The exposure to the world only reinforced his opinion of himself that he was a lesser person than those around him. Adopting this belief internally was anathema to his soul.

This leaves us with the dilemma of attempting to correct the need of those to bully others, hopefully while they are still young, so that they face the consequences of their behavior and are held to account for it while there still exists the need for them to develop self appreciation and the confidence that will allow them to be healthy citizens who contribute to the society and feel good about themselves as adults.

There Are Bullies In
The Animal Kingdom, Too!

Reinforcement of my belief that only individuals that feel inferior to their peers are often the ones who bully others was demonstrated by one of my homebred horses. The two broodmares I first bred on my farm were half-sisters that were sent to the same stallion.

After both were bred, the veterinarian predicted the delivery dates for both mares, which were only days apart. The first mare to deliver a colt was only a day after her predicted due date.

The other mare contracted a lung infection during her ninth month of pregnancy. A horse's gestation period is eleven months. The farm vet treated her and left me needles and syringes to inject her twice a day with penicillin and pills which I had to crush and suspend in water to flush down her throat four times a day. And each week for a month she had to be shipped to the veterinary clinic to have the catheter that was inserted into one side of her neck moved to the other side so a different antibiotic could be used in her treatment.

This must have been very traumatic for the mare, as during her treatment, she stopped eating and her teat bag filled with milk two months too early. That meant that the foal could be born at any time. Chances were that a premature foal would not survive; never mind growing up to become a racehorse. That wasn't exactly a great beginning for a new foal you hope will grow to be a winner. The vet told me there was nothing to do if the foal was born too early. There were no foal incubators at that time. After all the mare and I had gone through, I had to find a way to make her eat or she'd lose the foal.

I had read, in what was considered, "the Bible" of harness racing, *The Care And Training Of The Trotter And Pacer*, that a trainer whose horse refused to eat, spread a tarp in the horse's stall and put everything a horse might eat on the tarp to allow the horse to choose what she wanted. I had been feeding both pregnant mares a high protein feed to assure that the foals would grow strong and muscular, but I wasn't about to quibble if I could get the sick mare to eat something, *anything*; so she wouldn't lose the foal.

As a last resort, I tried what the trainer in the book had done. I laid a tarp in her stall and laid everything a horse might eat on top of it. The only things she chose to eat were beet pulp and carrots. After feeding her those two things, her milk bag reabsorbed but a month passed beyond the mare's due date and she still hadn't foaled.

That the mare was overdue raised new problems. The vet told me that if she didn't give birth by the day on which she was bred a year earlier, he would have to induce labor, which carries its own threats to both the mare and the foal. Three days before that date, the mare delivered a small, scrawny colt, who, unlike his cousin, did not romp and play but refused to leave his mother's side.

Both foals were weaned from their dams in the fall and have stayed together on the racetrack, in the field and finally, on the same farm after their retirement from racing.

The first born was bigger, faster, won more races and earned much more money on the track. He developed some trouble in his left hind ankle, but each time he heard the bugler call the horses to the post, his ears went up, he would arch his neck and proudly head to the starting gate. He might come back limping after the race, but he was always ready to meet the challenge and most often, he finished either first or second in the race.

The smaller, younger horse, was actually the first to win a race. But if anything, even the tiniest thing, ever bothered him, he'd try to wimp out of going to the gate to race. He might win a qualifying race when moved to a new track, but then he'd back up in the real, parimutuel race, when the purse money was on the line.

When the horses had the inside of their upper lips tattooed (A requirement, so that state stewards can identify that the horse is actually the one entered in the race), the first born stood staunchly and let the needle and the ink permanently identify him. When it was the smaller, younger one's turn to be tattooed, he shivered and shook and tried to duck away.

But who became the bully in the field? Who bit and kicked at any other horses who were in the field with him? Who kicked the cow on the farm where both horses went after they were retired? Which horse was the one to threaten the other horses away from their food if they happened to be fed first in the field? The smaller, younger one, of course!

Having been weak and fearful as a youngster, he had to be the one to threaten others as an adult, for fear that they would pick on him. It was on my farm that I realized that many of the behaviors I thought of as human were actually shared by other species.

I was reminded of this one summer, while in college, when I got a job in the primate house in the Central Park zoo for credit in my Anthropology course. In the rhesus monkey cage one monkey's facial features actually resembled those of people with Down Syndrome. He wasn't as active as the other monkeys in the cage and he also did not interact with others as much. The other monkeys threw pieces of fruit at him and sometimes smacked him as they swung by where he was perched. A female in the cage, though I had no clue to any familial connection, seemed to "mother" him; hugging him to her chest and attempting to push others away when they came near.

Being different from one's peers, whether smaller or weaker, or less active or not as smart, seems to draw rejection from which the target suffers. After years of feeling different and/or less able or important, it seems logical that such a person in a situation in which they finally feel more powerful than another, might lash out.

So What Do We Do Now?

In the years before social media, students who appeared weak or shy were often targets of bullies in school. Once they returned home from school, those who had been the targets of bullies had a reprieve from the taunts or worse. Now, through social media, those same students are vulnerable to even more bullying at home; through their phones or computers. The taunts may seem never ending; which is why I believe the incidence of teen suicide has sky rocketed in recent years.

An article by David Luxton, Jennifer June and Johnathan Fairall in the "American Journal Of Public Health" in 2012 evaluated 75 published studies on the topic and defined cyberbullying as intentionally and repeatedly targeting another child or teen with threats, harassment, humiliation or embarrassment by using cell phones, email, texting, social networking sites or instant messaging. Their study found that since the introduction of the Internet, the teens who use the technologies described above are twice as likely to attempt suicide.

During prepubescence and teenage years, individuals appear to be seeking their place in the pecking order of their peers. This is not limited to the human species. Young lions and tigers do it as well as various species of primates and I have personally witnessed it in the young horses I, myself, have raised.

It is their human peers that bullies seek to impress, as they believe their standing within the group will be enhanced by subjugating others. A good peer review is the most significant thing bullies seek to achieve. Therefore, proposal number one involves peer review; as peer evaluation is of primary importance to those who seek to bully others. Those who bully may not even be aware of the fact that their behavior exposes them to others as lacking in self worth.

Prepubescents and teenagers feel the need to bully others when they have low self esteem and feelings of inferiority. They seek to taunt, insult, "put down" and sometimes even assault those who appear weaker than themselves in an effort to enhance their social status with their peers. Both positive and negative reinforcement should be used to help alter their behavior and build self esteem while they are still young enough to make meaningful changes in their self worth. The key to success in curbing bullying behavior is not just intervening in it but in building self confidence in those who feel inferior at the same time.

Various individuals in the young lives of these people are capable of helping them make this transition. I believe that it begins with their peers, as they are the ones the bullies seek to impress; probably never realizing that their bullying behaviors are advertising the very weaknesses they feel and their attempts to cover that up. Those with the knowledge and wisdom of human behavior can discern it, nonetheless.

SIX PROPOSALS TO COUNTER
BULLYING IN
MIDDLE SCHOOL
AND HIGH SCHOOL

Proposal Number One
Peer Council Review

It is my suggestion that middle and high school administrators, with input from teachers, choose two outstanding students from each grade and three from the highest grade to be members of a "peer council". Members would be determined by their good grades and good behavior as well as their willingness to remain after school one day each week to address the bullying behavior of their student peers. Of course, parental consent would be necessary for those chosen to stay late after classes and to participate on the council.

The steps involved could look something like this:

> 1. Slips could be sent home with potential council members to explain the purpose of the council and to ask for the parent's permission for their children to participate.

2. The students on the peer council would interview both the alleged bully and the subject who reported the event together.

3. Then, members of the council would decide upon a course of action to remedy the situation. They could choose to do nothing or assign some task to a student they believe bullied another, like cleaning up the lunchroom or emptying the class trash can, etc. and determine the length of time needed to reinforce the sanction.

4. If the council felt the bully was in need of remediation to build his or her self-confidence, they could assign a tutor for help with classwork or refer the student to the school guidance counselor, etc. in order to build the student's self-worth.

5. In order to review these incidences of bullying by the peer council, suggestion boxes could be placed at various locations throughout the school. (The purpose and placement of these boxes would be known to all students and staff.) Alongside the boxes, pre-printed slips of paper would need to be available. These pre-printed slips would have spaces to indicate the date, time, location, bully and target

or witness. Slips would be replaced as needed.

By adopting such a process, anyone could report an incident of bullying behavior, be it a student who was the target of a bully or a witness to the event, and they could do so without any other person needing to know who reported the incident. This would preclude any retaliation upon those who might otherwise be regarded as "snitches" and the reporter could remain anonymous. Incidents to be evaluated by the peer council could happen within the school, on school grounds, at a school event, on the school bus or at home through social media.

6. Slips from inside each suggestion box would be collected by a member of the peer council at the end of each school day.

7. The teachers of those students whose names were written on the slips would then be advised at the end of classes on the day the peer council met, and those students would remain after classes were over to meet with the council. This would allow the teacher time to notify parents about where their children would be after the day's classes were over.

8. At the weekly peer council meeting, each student whose name was listed on a slip as a bully would be asked to describe the event in question, in their own words, and the reporter of the event, whether student or adult, would give their version.

9. A possible resolution to the event might be as simple as an apology, or an agreement that there had been a misunderstanding, or a promise that such behavior would not occur again.

10. If a simple solution was not evident, members of the peer council should decide in private what the corrective course of action should be. Such action could be anything from clearing lunchroom tables, emptying classroom wastebaskets or serving detention after school.

11. The decision of the peer council would then be made known to the attendees of the meeting, the teachers of the students involved and to the parents of the students who were to be reprimanded.

12. Any student involved could appeal the decision of the peer council directly to the head of the school.

In my opinion, it is not the action the council metes out to the student they decide exhibited bullying behavior that might bring about true change; it is the mere fact that the bully's own peers decide that he or she is at fault that changes the dynamics. The bully would be put on notice and realize that his or her peers were watching. The bully would have lost face in the eyes of those he or she most sought to impress; their peers! This is the exact opposite of what they hoped to achieve by bullying in the first place. That is why I believe implementing a peer council review process to address bullying can be a very powerful deterrent to future bullying behavior.

Proposal Number Two
Teacher Involvement

Should there be a repeat of bullying behavior by a student already reprimanded by the peer council, a student who satisfied what the council thought to be fair atonement but then later engaged in bullying behavior; or a student who refused to comply with the decision of the peer review council, that student would need to meet with his or her homeroom teacher.

The teacher would then need to explain to the student how significant his or her bullying behavior was and what it could lead to in the future, both socially and academically. The teacher would then need to ask the student for a dated, written, commitment that such behavior would not happen in the future and sign that he or she had been counseled by the teacher. The teacher would also need to notify the student that if such a recurrence happened, the student's parents would be notified and asked to attend a meeting at which everyone involved would work to create a plan to curb the student's bullying behaviors going forward, both at school *and at home.*

Sometimes, teachers of students with low opinions of themselves, can help their students bolster their confidence and belief in themselves by assigning these students class responsibilities such attendance taker, class monitor, or any other similar assignment. If teachers actively demonstrate that they trust their students to carry out assigned responsibilities, their students might conclude that they *must* have value and character traits worthy of recognition. And when these students *are* successful, they will receive positive recognition from an adult who is in charge, and possibly, acknowledgment from their peers as a result.

Proposal Number Three
Parental Involvement

If the first two proposals have not succeeded in curbing a student's penchant for bullying others, the parents *must* be called to the school to meet with the teacher and the student to create a plan to eliminate such behaviors. At that meeting, the parents would be informed of the prior two events in which their child bullied another (if they were not already aware of that), and the steps that had been taken by the school to address those behaviors.

At this meeting, the parents should be advised, in front of their child, of the possible social discrimination their child could face from peers. In addition, the student should be asked, in front of the parents, why he or she believed they could not stop such bullying behaviors. Then the parents and the student should each be asked how they plan to address the situation at home.

One option could be limited computer or television time. Or their phones could be taken away. A curfew might be imposed. The student could be banned from social media at home. The teacher should also ask how he or she could support the efforts of the parents.

A warning should also be given by the teacher to the student and the parents. This warning needs to stipulate that continuing with bullying behavior by the student will result in a referral to the school psychologist or counselor. (Should the student continue to bully others after working with the school psychologist or counselor, the student would be referred to the head of the school for more focused disciplinary action such as suspension or expulsion.)

Dated notes would need to be taken by the teacher that included all relevant statements and plans by all the participants, and these notes would be placed in the student's permanent record file. Both the parents and the student would then need to be advised that these notes would follow the student to whatever educational facility he or she might subsequently attend.

The fact that a student may not be able to curtail his or her tendency to taunt, humiliate or attack others may seem odd to some but I, myself have witnessed it with the students Joe and Maria, about whom I've already written. Joe called Maria stupid and ugly and said she'd never make any friends. (A classic case of projection, not unlike that of the former President.)

Though Joe was not fond of staying after school, one afternoon he just stood up and announced,"I'm tired of staying after school every day! I'm not going to insult that girl anymore!" and he didn't.

So it seems that given some consequence, even stubborn students can change their behavior. Joe stopped insulting Maria completely and without any further word from me. He just got tired of being punished!

Proposal Number Four
Involving the School Psychologist

Should a student persist in exhibiting bullying behaviors beyond being involved in the first three proposals, I believe that his or her underlying feelings of inferiority may be severe and outside the norms of the average bully. In my opinion, that requires some form of professional mental help that can be administered by the school psychologist. The psychologist, after being advised by the student's teacher and reading the notes in the student's permanent file, should set up a schedule to meet with the student several times a week. The counselor should feel free to explore with the student why he or she is so angry, frustrated and feels so different from others.

The psychologist should begin by asking the student to describe his or her version of the incidences of bullying that were identified by other students and adults. In this way, the counselor is able to determine if the student can determine past actions factually or if the student always sees himself or herself as a victim. The student should also be asked why he or she feels the need to persist in what others identify as bullying behavior.

The counselor could seek to determine the cause of the student's need to feel better about himself or herself by asking questions like did he or she ever feel bullied at home? Is anyone in school bullying him or her? Is there anyone who is making this student feel frightened or bad about themselves? What is home life like?

In this way, the psychologist may identify the cause of this student's need to put others down and possibly remediate it. The student should also be advised that if the bullying behavior continues to persist, the counselor will have no choice but to refer the student to the Principal or Headmaster for possible suspension or even expulsion.

Proposal Number Five
Involving the
Principal or Headmaster

Should the same student who exhibits bullying behavior not be dissuaded from doing so after being interviewed by the peer council, meeting with the homeroom teacher, participating in a meeting with both a parent and the teacher and being counseled by the school psychologist, he or she must meet with the school Principal or Headmaster.

Prior to this meeting, the Principal or Headmaster will have reviewed this student's personal record file so that the Principal is aware of all the interventions that have been attempted.

At this meeting, the Principal or Headmaster should ask the student why all the prior attempts to stop the bullying behavior have failed. The student should be asked directly, why he or she still feels the need to attack others and what can be done to change this behavior. The key here, as far as helping this student, is for the Principal or Headmaster to demonstrate sincere concern for the welfare of the student.

That said, the student would also need to be advised that if there were no change in their behavior going forward, discilinary steps would need to be implemnted. Several options exist for the Principal or Headmaster at this point, including lunch detention, after-school detention, in-school suspension, out-of-school suspension, and even expulsion. The precise disciplinary action taken will depend upon several factors (the age of the student, the severity of the bullying incidents, and whether the student exhibits any remorse).

Finally, if none of the above work to deter bullying behavior, the Principal or Headmaster may seek the assistance of the School's Resource Officer (SRO) as the next step.

Proposal Number Six
Involving Law Enforecment

Should the student still engage in bullying behavior after going through the five previous steps, it is time for law enforcement to get involved. Many schools already have police liaisons, called School Resource Officers. Many Middle Schools and most High Schools in the Commonwealth have an SRO, and some schools have more than one.

At this stage, the school's SRO should interview the recalcitrant student about all prior incidents of bullying behaviors. The officer should make the student aware of what a lifetime of targeting others could lead to. (Think of what is now happening to Donald Trump.)

Then, unless there are direct criminal charges to be filed, the officer should assign the student to after-school community service. The student could be assigned to work at a

community shelter for the homeless. Or at a
community pantry, serving meals to others.
Or at a group home, assisting others less
fortunate. Or any other similar community
service where the student serves others.

I have found that bullies can begin to see
themselves as"helpful" and "good"after they
have spent some time serving others who are
truly less fortunate. They can see themselves
as contributing to society when they begin
working with people who are actually lower
on the social totem pole than they are. In this
way, they prove to themselves that they *do*
have value, and their self-esteem soars. And
as their positive image of themselves grows,
their need to put others down lessens.

Of course, any act of bullying that
involves actual violence, or a credible threat
of violence, rather than just taunts or insults,
may be criniminal in nature. The SRO should
be contacted immediately.

My Hope For This Book

I have proposed a six-tiered plan to address the bullying behaviors of prepubescent and teenage students. It is a plan I hope schools will adopt. Yes, I understand that every school district has plans already in place to address behavior issues; but I also think that many times we as educators, administrators, and parents, lose sight of the internal dynamics of those who bully others, and so we miss the best way to help them change their behaviors. I hope that my book, my proposals, if you will, will facilitate this change. I hope that these specific proposals can lead to the building of self-esteem in those who, for whatever reason, feel inferior to others, and that by helping them embrace a more positive self-image, they will abandon their need to bully others in order to feel better about themselves.

No one likes to think of themselves as "bad" or "evil"; so if the target of the bully seems dismissive of such behavior, the bully's belief that he or she is still "good" can lead the bully to feel better about himself and grateful to the would be target for reinforcing that feeling. If one can meet a bully's threats with a nonchalant shrug, revealing neither fear nor anger nor defiance, with the target basically seeming to be unaffected by the threats, that may help the bully to actually feel better about himself.

Defying the bully by demonstrating no fear in the face of a threat of physical harm may make the target of the bully feel empowered, but it runs the risk of enraging the bully, who may actually carry out the harm he or she has threatened. Of all the possible reactions to the threats of bullies, in my experience, those kinds of unremarkable responses have proved to produce the best outcomes for both targets and bullies.

Along with the peers of bullies, teachers, parents, school psychologists and administrators may all contribute valuable input that can change the self images of those who feel the need to bully others. Assigning the right sorts of responsibilities (not overwhelming ones) to those who feel the need to bully, can lead them to build their self images and self esteem. If all those efforts fail, in extreme cases, local law enforcement liaisons can assign persistent bullies to community service that may lead to success when other efforts to curtail their bullying behaviors have failed.

As many plans as can be imagined that emphasize both positive and negative reinforcements should be employed to help these students adjust so that they display only acceptable social behaviors. Making these students aware of their psychological needs may also help them accept their inner feelings and assist them in understanding that their bullying behaviors will not help them achieve the enhanced social status they seek nor will it ultimately allow them to feel better about themselves.

In addition to the steps to address specific instances of bullying, teachers can take time to present alternatives to entire classes by having them role play past incidents of bullying they either witnessed or experienced and asking the class how the incident might have played out differently. Students can explore suggestions made by classmates and see how those adopted suggestions could have changed the outcome of such incidents. Negative feelings about one's self can also be discussed with suggestions of other ways than suicide to address one's self-deprecation by the students in the class to help other students realize that there are different ways to encourage self-worth and self-confidence.

Appendix A
Pennsylvania Anti-Bullying Laws
And Policies

The information on the following pages was collected and forwarded to the author by several individuals including staff from the Office of Pennsylvania State Representative Thom Welby, and Drew Popish, the Chief of Staff for State Representative Bridget Kozierowski.

Components of State Anti-Bullying Laws and Regulations

Component	Included
Prohibiting Statement	No
Definition	Yes
Scope	Yes
Protected Groups	No
District Policy Requirement	Yes
Reporting and Investigations	Yes
Consequences	Yes
Communication of Policy	Yes
Safeguards and Supports	No
Review/Update Local Policies	Yes
Prevention Education	Yes
Staff Training	Yes
Parent Engagement	No

Which Pennsylvania Laws and Regulations Cover Bullying?

Pennsylvania Statute 24#13-1302A.
    Office for Safe Schools
Pennsylvania Statute 24#13-1303-A.
    Reporting
Pennsylvania Statute 24#13-1303.1-A.
    Policy relating to bullying
Pennsylvania Statute 24#13-1306-B.
    School Safety and Security Grant
    Program

Pennsylvania Statute 24#13-1309-B.
    School Safety and Security Coordinator
Pennsylvania Statute 24#13-1310-B.
    School Safety and Security Training
Pennsylvania Consolidated Statute 18#2801.
    Definitions
Pennsylvania Consolidated Statute 18#2802.
    Hazing
Pennsylvania Consolidated Statute 18#2803.
    Aggregated Hazing
Pennsylvania Consolidated Statute 18#2804.
    Organizational Hazing
Pennsylvania Consolidated Statute 18#2805.
    Institutional Hazing
Pennsylvania Consolidated Statute 18#2806.
    Defenses Prohibited
Pennsylvania Consolidated Statute 18#2807.
    Forfeiture
Pennsylvania Consolidated Statute 18#2808.
    Enforcement By Institution or
    Secondary School
Pennsylvania Consolidated Statute 18#209.
    Institutional Reports
Pennsylvania Consolidated Statute 18#2810.
    Safe Harbor
Pennsylvania Consolidated Statute 18#2811.
    Civil Remedies

How are Bullying and Cyberbullying Defined in Pennsylvania?

Pennsylvania anti-bullying laws include the following definitions of bullying and cyberbullying:

Bullying shall mean an intentional electronic, written verbal or physical act,

or a series of acts:

(1) directed at another student or students;

(2) which occurs in a school setting;

(3) that is severe, persistent or pervasive; and

(4) that has the effect of doing any of the following:

   (i)   substantially interfering with a student's education;

   (ii) creating a threatening environment

   (iii) substantially disrupting the orderly operation of the school

24 Pa. Stat.#13-1303.1-A (2008)

Purdon's Pennsylvania Statutes and Consolidated Statutes Title 24 P.S. Education (Effective July 1, 2008)

Policy Relating to Bullying

#13-1303.1-A Effective July 1, 2008

Chapter 1. Public School Code of 1949

(Refs &Annos)

Article XIII-a Safe Schools (Refs& Annos)
Effective July 1, 2008
Currentness
(a) No later than January 1, 2009, each
student entity shall adopt a policy or
amend its existing policy relating to
bullying and incorporate the policy into
the school entity's code of student conduct
required under 22 Pa. Code #12.3(c)
(relating to school rules).

The policy shall delineate disciplinary
consequences for bullying and may
provide for prevention, intervention and
education programs, provided that no
school entity shall be required to establish
a new policy under this section if one
currently exists and reasonably fulfills the
requirements of this section. The policy
shall identify the appropriate school staff
person to receive reports of incidents of
alleged bullying.

(b) Each school entity shall make the
policy available on its publicly accessible
internet website, if available, and in every
classroom. Each school entity shall post
the policy in a prominent location within
each school building where such notices
are usually posted. Each school entity shall

ensure that the policy and procedures for reporting bullying incidents are reviewed with students within ninety (90) days after their adoption and thereafter at least once each school year.

(c) Each school entity shall review its policy every three (3) years and annually provide the office with a copy of its policy relating to bullying, including information related to development and implementation of any bullying prevention, intervention and education programs. The information required under this subsection shall be attached to or made part of the annual report required under section 1303-A(b)

(d) In its policy relating to bullying adopted or maintained under subsection (a), a school entity shall not be prohibited from defining bullying in such a way as to encompass acts that occur outside a school setting if those acts meet the requirements contained in subsection (e) (1), (3) and (4). If a school entity reports acts of bullying to the office in accordance with section 1303-A (b), it shall report all incidents that qualify as bullying under the entity's adopted definition of that term.

(e) For purposes of this article, "bullying" shall mean an intentional electronic, written, verbal or physical act, or a series of acts:

(1) directed at another student or students;

(2) which occurs in a school setting;

(3) that is severe, persistent and pervasive; and

(4) that has the effect of doing any of the following:

(i) substantially interfering with a student's education;

(ii) creating a threatening environment; or

(iii) substantially disrupting the orderly operation of the school; and "school setting" shall mean in the school, on school grounds, in school vehicles, at a designated bus stop or at any activity sponsored, supervised or sanctioned by the school.

Current through 2022 Regular Session Act 97.

Appendix B
Frequently Asked Questions

Do Pennsylvania Anti-Bullying Laws and Regulations Cover Cyberbullying That Occurs Off Campus?

Yes. Pennsylvania anti-bullying laws state that a school entity shall not be prohibited from defining bullying in such a way as to encompass acts that occur outside a school setting if those acts meet the requirements contained in the bullying definition in state law.

What Are the Policy Requirements for Schools to Prevent and Respond to Bullying Behavior?

Pennsylvania school districts must adopt a policy or amend existing policies related to bullying and must incorporate the policy in the school entity's code of conduct. School district policies must contain key policy and procedural elements, including but not limited to:

1. Definitions of bullying;
2. Disciplinary consequences for violation of the policy;
3. Designation of an appropriate school staff person to receive reports of incidents of alleged bullying;
4. Procedures for reporting bullying incidents; and Requirements regarding

how the policy will be publicized within the district.

5. Pennsylvania anti-bullying laws require school districts to review bullying policies every three years and annually to provide the Office for Safe Schools with a copy of the policy, including information related to the development and implementation of any bullying prevention, intervention and education programs. Pennsylvania anti-bullying laws also require districts to report to the Office of Safe Schools all incidents that qualify as bullying under the school district's adopted definition of the term and that meet requirements for state reporting.

Do Pennsylvania Anti-Bullying Laws and Regulations Include Protection for Specific Groups?

No. There are no specific groups listed under Pennsylvania anti-bullying laws or regulations. Pennsylvania schools that receive Federal funding are required by federal law to address discrimination based on certain personal characteristics. *Find out when bullying may be a civil rights violation.*

Do Pennsylvania Anti-Bullying Laws and Regulations Encourage or Require

Districts to Implement Bullying Prevention Programs or Strategies?

Yes. Pennsylvania anti-bullying laws encourage districts to provide for prevention, intervention and education programs in school bully policies. Pennsylvania anti-bullying laws also direct the state Office for Safe Schools to make targeted grants to school entities to fund the development and implementation of research-based violence prevention programs that address risk factors to reduce incidents of problem behaviors among students including, but not limited to, bullying. Pennsylvania anti-bullying laws also require each school entity to to appoint a school safety and security coordinator who is responsible for coordinating training and resources for students and school entity staff in matters relating to bullying awareness.

Do Pennsylvania Anti-Bullying Laws and Regulations Encourage or Require Districts to Train Teachers and Other School Staff on How to Respond to Bullying Incidents?

Yes. Pennsylvania anti-bullying laws require school entities to provide employees with mandatory training on school safety and security including training addressing suicide and bullying awareness.

Do Pennsylvania Anti-Bullying Laws and Regulations Encourage or Require Districts to Provide Safeguards or Mental Health Supports for Students Involved with Bullying?

No. Pennsylvania anti-bullying laws do not require districts to provide safeguards or mental health supports for students involved with bullying.

Do Pennsylvania Anti-Bullying Laws and Regulations Involve Parents in Efforts to Address Bullying Behavior?

No. Pennsylvania anti-bullying laws do not create expectations for parent involvement in addressing bullying.

For more information, please visit the Pennsylvania Department of Education's "Bullying Prevention" web page on bullying and harassment. The key component framework used in the analysis of state laws is based on the review of legislation presented in the "Analysis of State Bullying Laws and Policies-December 2011" (U.S. Department of Education). Date Last Reviewed: August 1, 2021.

Appendix C
Additional Resources and
Other Information

Bullying Prevention

The Pennsylvania Department of Education's Office for Safe Schools bullying prevention webpage contains resources for parents, educators and professionals serving children and youth in school and out-of-school settings.

Bullying Prevention Consultation Line
1-866-716-0424

The toll free Bullying Prevention Consultation Line invites individuals experiencing chronic and unresolved bullying to discuss effective strategies and available resources to manage school-based bullying.

This resource was developed in collaboration with the Center for Health Promotion and Disease Prevention (CHPDP), and is available at no cost to students, parents/guardians and school districts across Pennsylvania. Messages left will be returned during normal business hours Monday through Friday.

Please note: this number is not monitored 24 hours a day/seven days a week and should not be used for emergencies. Watch the PA Bullying Prevention Consultation Line Video (You Tube)

Funding
Access information on Safe Schools Targeted
Grants.

Resources

1. *A School Guide to Developing an Action Plan for Students Who May Be Bullied*
Waiting to develop an action plan for a
student who may be bullied can place
a student at risk. Learn best practices on how
to implement this Tier 3 strategy. Research
suggests that using a multi-tiered comprehensive approach to bullying prevention
is most effective. This resource describes
how bullying prevention practices can be
integrated into a school's PBIS system or
other tiered systems of support.

2. *Center for Health Promotion and Disease Prevention*
The Center for Health Promotion and Disease
Prevention (CHPDP), along with its existing
local, regional, national and international
partnerships, serves as a model U.S. health
program. The Center staff members are
dedicated to prevention, health promotion
and wellness, as well as the identification of
positive changes in behavior and health for

the citizens of our community. The CHPDP implements evidence-based initiatives with the goal of improving the health of the children and adults we serve. They monitor and evaluate all of their programs to determine project impact. Their dedicated staff has authored and co-authored, along with the Highmark Foundation, several comprehensive publications and journal articles to report our program outcomes.

3. *The Committee for Children*
The Mission Statement of this committe is as follows: "To foster the safety and well-being of children through social-emotional learning and development. Covid-19 Response: Find new on-demand teacher-led lessons, videos and free resources for educators, students and families. Topics include SEL, Second Step middle-school remote learning advisory guide, lessons and activities.

4. *Common Sense Media*
Since 2003, Common Sense has been the leading source of entertainment and technology recommendations for families and schools. Every day, millions of parents and educators trust Common Sense reviews and advice to help them navigate the digital world with their kids. Together with policy makers,

industry leaders and global media partners, we're building a digital world that works better for all kids, their families and their communities.

5. *Teaching "Digital Citizenship" (K-12)*
This online resource includes lesson plans on topics such as "Finding Balance in a Digital World" and "Who Are You Online?"

6. *Cyberbullying Research Institute*
The Cyberbullying Research Institute is dedicated to providing up-to-date information about the nature, extent, causes and consequences of cyberbullying among adolescents. Their website features online cyberbullying resources for parents, educators and youth. Their website also features online resources on topics such as Online Learning, Social isolation and cyberbullying: *How to Support Our Students.*

7. *Facing History and Ourselves*
Uses lessons from history to challenge teachers and their students to stand up to bigotry and hate.

8. *Making Caring Common*
A project of the Harvard Graduate School of Education. Their Mission Statement is

as follows: "Our vision is a world in which children learn to care about others and the common good, treat people well day to day, come to understand and seek fairness and justice, and do what is right even at times at a cost to themselves. We believe young people with these capacities will become community members and citizens who can strengthen our democracy, mend the fractures that divide us and create a more caring, just world."

9. *Pacer Center*
From their Mission Statement: "The PACER Center enhances the quality of life and expands opportunities for children, youth and young adults with all disabilities and their families so each person can reach his or her highest potential. PACER operates on the principles of parents helping parents, supporting families, promoting a safe environment for all children and working in collaboration with others."

10. *Onspire Learning Network*
An online educational service provided by Educational Department Software (EDS) – a company that specializes in student support programs helping students and supporting educators. EDS is proud to serve over 1700 schools in PA, NJ, TX and MS and continues

to maintain its singular focus – creating comprehensive, effective learning solutions for K – 12 schools. From online reporting systems to evidence supported online professional development opportunities, EDS focuses on anti-bullying reporting and management, intervention programs and student assistance.

11. *Pennsylvania Bullying Prevention Toolkit* Resources for parents, educators and professionals serving children, youth and families.

12. *Safe2Say Something* Safe2Say Something is a youth violence prevention program run by the Pennsylvania Office of Attorney General. The program teaches youth and adults how to recognize warning signs and signals, especially within social media, from individuals who may be a threat to themselves or others and to say something **BEFORE** it is too late. With Safe2Say Something, it's easy and confidential to report safety concerns to help prevent violence and tragedies.

13. *StopBullying.gov* StopBullying.gov provides information from various government agencies on what bullying is, what cyberbullying is, who is at

risk and how you can prevent and respond to bullying.

14. *STOPit Solutions*
STOPit Solutions is an anonymous reporting and help system that provides students state-of-the-art tools to get help for themselves and others. Over 6,000 K-12 schools nationwide use STOPit; helping thousands of students and school communities each day.

15. *The School for Ethical Education (SEE)*
Teaches strategies to put ethics in action for positive student character formation.

Webinars
1. *Bullying Prevention and Social Emotional Learning (SEL): What Can I Do Now?*
Presenter: Leah Galkowski, Safe Schools Coordinator, Center for Safe Schools

2. *Meeting the Challenge of Bullying Prevention in a Digital Learning Environment*
Presenters from the Olweus Bullying Prevention Program (OBPP) share ideas for establishing a safe, welcoming virtual classroom and discuss how to promote social connection with physical distance.

3. *School Health Spotlights from the Center for Health Promotion and Disease Prevention*

School Health Spotlights are online continuing education sessions featuring community health professionals. Spotlight topics reflect current school health issues for schools, parents and caregivers, and student-serving professionals such as three tiers for bullying prevention, cyberbullying and meaningful bullying prevention, among other topics.

Appendix D
An Afterword

A Comparison of the Six Proposals to Address Bullying to the Existing Pennsylvania Laws and Regulations Regarding Bullying

After reviewing the collection of state laws, policies and regulations already enacted, it is evident that Pennsylvania takes the subject of bullying seriously. The Commonwealth has invested much time, energy and research into strategies to combat such behavior with its definitions, policies and regulations; online suggestions, webinars and a commitment to making these laws, policies and regulations clearly visible to students, teachers, other school staffers and administrators.

A clear, demonstrable difference between the existing state laws, policies and regulations that address bullying in Pennsylvania and the six proposals recommended in this handbook; are that students, the peers of the alleged bully, are included in addressing the bullying behavior and are the first to do so. In most cases, they are the ones the bully seeks to impress. Not only does having the bully's peers hear and decide upon consequences that can potentially embarrass the bully and allow him or her to see that his or her strategy is not working to serve the purpose of the bullying behavior, but it also allows young people to address serious threats in which they are involved and propose solutions to solve those threats. What better preparation for adult life?

In addition, the parents of the alleged bully are also involved in a direct way. They can enact strategies at home that can reinforce what student peers and teachers of the alleged bully have already tried to accomplish. In the state's proposals, parents/legal guardians/persons legally in control of the alleged bully are only notified of such alleged behavior or can let school administrators know if their child has endured a reported incident of bullying. The direct involvement of parents in this plan may further help to accomplish a change in the alleged bully's behavior.

Similarly, there is some recognition that a mental problem might exist as the cause behind some forms of bullying behavior and the state of Pennsylvania refers to the possibility of counseling for the alleged bully but in this handbook, the specific step of involving the school psychologist is part and parcel of the increasing steps to address repeated bullying behavior. This step can be crucial to changing the understanding of the alleged bully and even effect change in his or her behavior.

Additionally, according to the state's proposals, there is no specific time at which the school's law enforcement officer (the SRO) becomes involved with the alleged bully's behavior. It is only one of many choices the state has in dealing with the alleged bully's behavior. In the six step approach outlined in this handbook, the SRO's involvement is the most serious and his or her decision as to what consequence to impose upon the alleged bully may make all the difference in changing his or her behavior.

Also, nowhere in the state's laws, policies, regulations or proposals have I encountered the suggestion that alleged bullies serve time in community service. Seeing that other people may have a harder life than the alleged bully allows them not to feel so sorry for themselves and offers them the opportunity to actually help others and be seen as the generous, helpful, "good" person;

something they may have never experienced before. This alone can change the perception of the alleged bully and can be the reason for him or her to change their behavior.

If schools throughout the state of Pennsylvania adopt the proposals offered in this handbook, I truly believe that changing the behavior of bullies can be accomplished while the students are still young enough to become productive, competent, contributing members of adult society. They can feel better about themselves and lead a life content with their own values.

ABOUT THE AUTHOR

Sherry Skramstad was a special education teacher for thirty-three years. She holds a Bachelors degree and a Masters Degree in Special Education from the City College of New York. Ms. Skramstad has taught in public elementary schools, middle schools, in two New York State prisons and at the Job Corps in Callicoon, New York.

In addition to her teaching experience, Ms. Skramstad served in the Publicity Departments of three major harness racetracks (Monticello Raceway, Goshen Historic Track and Pocono Downs) in the northeast. She was an owner/trainer/breeder of Standardbred racehorses and owned a horse farm in Woodbourne, NY where she bred her two Standardbred mares and then raised, broke, trained and campaigned their four offspring at racetracks and in Sire Stakes across the state of New York.

Ms. Skramstad worked as an Account Executive at WSUL radio in Monticello where she both sold air time and wrote commercials. She was the Executive Assistant for Friends and Advocates for Mental Health in Monticello and also served as the bookkeeper there as well as at H.T.S. Rack Company in Manhattan and as the Horsemen's bookkeeper at Monticello Raceway.

Early in her career, Ms. Skramstad did medical research for thirteen years; first working on a cure for cancer at the Bellevue NYU Medical Center and then on a cure for leukemia at Jewish Memorial Hospital; both in Manhattan.

In April of 2010, Ms. Skramstad had her first book published. It was entitled, *Wendy's Wisdom: The Challenges And Accomplishments Of A Woman With Down Syndrome*, which was written about her sister who was born in 1948. This book was re-issued in 2022 under the title *The Lucky Few: Celebrating the life and legacy of my sister, Wendy, a person with Down Syndrome*. Ms. Skramstad is also the author of the novel, *The Ladies' Catskill: A Murder Mystery*, published in 2021.

The author on the left with her sister, Wendy.